Dedicated to

John A. Mann Jr. and Rosalyn Johnston Mann

Thank you for teaching me to love history and family heritage.

FRONTIER MILITIA

THE WAR OF 1812

Timothy A. Mann

HERITAGE BOOKS

2011

HERITAGE BOOKS

AN IMPRINT OF HERITAGE BOOKS, INC.

Books, CDs, and more—Worldwide

For our listing of thousands of titles see our website
at
www.HeritageBooks.com

Published 2011 by
HERITAGE BOOKS, INC.
Publishing Division
100 Railroad Ave. #104
Westminster, Maryland 21157

Other books by the author:

Colonel John Mann, Jr.: His Kith, His Kin, His Ancestors, His Descendants
Revised Edition

International Standard Book Numbers
Paperbound: 978-0-7884-5336-6
Clothbound: 978-0-7884-8859-7

PREFACE

There has been little information has published about frontiersmen living in northwest Ohio at the commencement of the War of 1812. They are often overshadowed by prominent leaders of the day.... men such as Cass, Harrison, Tecumseh, and Winchester. The lives of these great leaders intersected the frontiersmen in northwest Ohio. Immediately after General Hull's disastrous campaign that ended in surrender at Detroit, the men in northwest Ohio were the front line of defense for both the state and the nation.

This book has been written to provide several snapshots of the Ohio Militia, its structure, a story that describe the dangers of living in what was considered a war zone, and some sites of significance in the state of Ohio during the war. Another main focus in this publication concerns the Fifth Division, as these men were stationed predominately throughout northwest Ohio. Unfortunately, their contribution to the war effort has been scantly recorded.

As this collection of documents has grown, I have been asked why I seem to focus on Miami County and the Fifth Division. At the commencement of the War of 1812, Miami County Ohio's southern boundary was the modern Miami/Montgomery county line, and Miami's northern boundary was the Ohio/Michigan state line. Miami also was responsible for the Darke County region at that time, as Darke did not officially become a county until 1817.........That's a lot of territory ....

I hope that the text within will be found useful to reenactors, researchers, and historians.

– T. Mann

3

TABLE OF CONTENTS

COUNTY MAP FOR THE STATE OF OHIO CIRCA 1812

The Wolverton Incident & The Dilbone Massacre

"The Wolverton Incident"

The first massacre concerning Miami County was not the Dilbone massacre, but an "incident" that happened one year prior.

A group of peaceful Indians were ambushed by Miami Militia. In a letter to the Liberty Hall Newspaper, General Edmund Munger noted that arms were being sent from Urbana to supply several parties of Miami's men. These men were to patrol the area between Greenville and the Piqua-Troy area. Major Charles Wolverton, who was in command of Fort Greenville, was on patrol with a company of men. An Indian camp was discovered near their post. Without attempting to determine the position or loyalties of these Indians, the company of men attacked the Indians. Two Indians were killed another wounded, and several captured. The Indians offered no resistance.

The May 1812 edition of the Ohio Centinel describes the "incident":

The Indians-The savages appear to be engaged on every quarter of our frontier in committing depredations upon the lives and property of settlers. On the 20th of last month, they killed and scalped a man near Greenville. In consequence of the murder of Greenville, a volunteer company of militia from Miami County marched to that neighborhood, and we have been notified that they killed two, wounded another and taken two squaws and a boy prisoner. They are in pursuit of the wounded Indian, and they state a determination to kill every Indian they meet with, until they have further orders.

A later edition of the Centinel states that the wounded Indian lost his hand do to the injury. Who were these Indians camping near Greenville? Unfortunately, they were a friendly hunting party. They were the family of an Indian named Killbuck. The surviving Indians were taken to the fort, kept for some time. They were later sent under guard to Colonel John Johnston, a Federal Indian Agent who resided in Piqua, Ohio.

Johnston personally took this family back to Greenville, and ordered the Militia to restore their property. He then released them to their tribe. Colonel Johnston's official report to the Secretary of War, William Eustice was as follows:

The Honorable William Eustice
Secretary of War
Piqua, Ohio

Sir,
Since writing you last, a detachment of Militia on duty at Greenville fell in with a party of friendly Indians. They killed two, wounded one, and took two women and a child prisoner. The Indians were quietly at their camp, unoffending and unresisting, not even having their guns loaded. On hearing of this affair, I repaired to the place, clamed the prisoners, and sent them home in the charge with some Shawnees with a suitable speech to the nation to which they belonged. A few days later came a party of Shawnees hunting in the same direction, which were taken by the Militia without opposition or bloodshed, they were sent to me and returned to their nation. I scarcely got clear of them when I received a message from the officer commanding the Militia that he had taken a mixed part of Indians, two Miami's, four Delaware men and women. Among these prisoners was the younger Killbuck who was suspected of being the murderer of Henry Rush, a citizen of the United States lately killed at Greenville. I found it necessary to proceed there in order to take testimony touching the case, accordingly took several depositions, and found strong grounds for suspicion. I sent young Killbuck under guard (having first dismissed the others with written speeches to their tribes) to the county prison to take his trial, and on the first night of their being on the road, the fellow ran away from the guard, and has not since been heard of. I had consented that his wife should accompany him and she remains in custody. I shall take the opportunity to send her home shortly. In consequence, of all the late murders by the savages, armed parties of our people are out in all directions breathing destruction against the Indians indiscriminately; the most fatal consequences would

ensued if some person had not been charged with the care and management of this quarter........

Life on the frontier was filled with violence for citizens in this area. It appears even more so for Indians. As for young Killbuck, he successfully escaped from his guard, and escaped a murder trial. Not all Indians were so lucky. Governor Meigs received an official report of the Wolverton Incident. It read as follows:

Montgomery County
May 14th, 1812

Sir-

In conformity to your orders of the 7th Instant, I have been at Greenville, and have examined the circumstances of the affair of killing two Indians near that place. By legal testimony, I find that those Indians were discovered by Captain Fish the evening before they were killed, he informed Major Wolverton and his party of the discovery. The next morning, the Major and ten men went in pursuit of the Indians, and found them at their camp. As soon as the Indians discovered Wolverton's party, they ran, and were fired upon by the Major's party. Two were killed, one wounded, two squaws and one child were taken prisoner. I understand by the witness, that there was no order given to fire at the time the Indians were killed, but the men had previous orders not to hurt squaws or children.

I likewise understood that the party with Major Wolverton had just seen the mangled corpse of one of their fellow citizens, who had fallen innocent victim to savage barbarity, without the least insult or provocation. This exasperated the men to such a degree, that it was very difficult to control them.

I was informed by Mr. Conner, a trader at Fort Recovery, that the party of Indians which were killed stayed at his house several days, and appeared to be friendly. They told him they were going to buy whiskey, they had a number of horses, and a considerable quantity of skins. They also had one handsome bridle with a plated bit, and one of their guns was stamped "London" on the barrel. Whether they are friends or foes is unknown, but they are of the Pottowattomie Nation.

We found on our arrival at Greenville five other Indians, who were in the possession of our party. they appeared to be friendly, and they were fearful that settlers might come across them and kill them. These Indians were of the Shawnee Nation. When I left Greenville, I thought it advisable to bring them all on with us, together with all their property, which I sent to Mr. Johnston, the Indian Agent, to dispose of agreeable to your directions.

I would further state to your Excellency the alarming situation of the settlements in the route we went. We found nearly all the inhabitants above the Stillwater River had evacuated their houses and farms, and removed back. We understand that if there could be a sufficient number of men sent on the frontier, they could go back and plant corn, and would return to their homes again.

I believe there is a probability of the Indians making an attack shortly. Mr. Conner told me that he had been advised by friendly Indians to remove from his place, or he would be killed, for the Prophet's party had determined to fall on the white peoples as soon as the leaves put out and their horses got in better order. He also said that there was a number of Indians at different times who related the same story. He has therefore removed to that place and was at Greenville. Everything looks like war with the Indians, although I believe some are determined not to act on either side.

If your Excellency should think proper to send out a detachment of men to those parts, to be stationed at such places as you may think proper to direct, under some vigilant officer. I would be leave to recommend Colonel Jerome Holt to be a man very suitable for that command, he having been an active officer, and thoroughly acquainted with all that part of the country, having served in all the different campaigns, through the last Indian War.

I have the Honor to be, with Respect,
Your Excellency's Most Obedient Humble Servant,
Edmund Munger, Brigadier General

Troy Citizens Petition the Governor

Miami County was an extremely dangerous place to live. Indian attacks were on the rise. Miami and Greene counties were considered war zone by the state, and men who stayed on their farms were draft exempt. Settlers in neighboring counties were being killed, and it was no surprise to settlers when murders occurred in this area. Prior to the Dilbone Massacre, thirty-five men from Troy petitioned Ohio's governor, R.J. Meigs concerning the Indians who were gathered at the Johnston Farm.

Miami County
State of Ohio
February 3, 1813

To His Excellency R.J. Meigs Governor of the said State

The petition of the undersigned humbly sheweth- that whereas there are a considerable number of Indians of the Delaware tribes called in by order of General Harrison, and are now in our county, that it is but thinly settled on the frontier, distant from a market where provisions can be furnished them. The people of the neighborhood, feel themselves in a dangerous situation in the consequences of their being exposed to invasion and depredation from them, they lying contiguous to the enemy, have every opportunity of conveying information to them of our situation, moving off and joining them and doing much mischief, from their knowledge of our country etc.etc.-

This brief petition we would humbly beg your Excellency to take into consideration and relieve us from a state of uneasiness and alarm, by having them removed to the interior of our state, where from its population they will be awed into the submission to the authorities having charge over them and supported at a much less expense to the Government.....

At the outset of hostilities, Colonel Johnston was the unofficial authority in the county. Johnston spent his time trying to keep peace with the Indian nations, provide safety and shelter for many Indians camping at his farm, and attempting to intervene in Militia "incidents". The latter was frustrating for him, as he had no official power or rank concerning the Ohio Militia. His pleas for assistance often went unanswered. Local history books state that Johnston wrote to George Buchanan, a Captain at a blockhouse in Covington. He appealed for help. This is true, however, Buchanan likely responded because he was also ordered by Governor Meigs to assist Johnston. In order to obtain this assistance, Johnston appealed in writing to the United States Secretary of War, William Eustice. Eustice appealed to Ohio's governor through contacts in Washington.

The Honorable William Eustice
Secretary of War Piqua, Ohio

Sir,
You will received intelligence from other sources that the British have taken Mackinac, and that as a natural consequence, General Hull has ordered Fort Dearborn at Chicago to be evacuated. The loss of these two very important establishments will give the enemy complete ascendancy over the Indians. I feel that this will be felt severely on our frontiers. I wrote to you some time since for an order on the Military Store at New Port, Kentucky, for 60 stands of arms, - 30 rifles, and 30 muskets. I entreat you to send it to me immediately for the safe keeping and to enable us to keep our ground here,. I will give any pledge for the safe keeping and due return of the arms which you may desire. I have all the Indian goods for Detroit, Sandusky, Fort Wayne, and this places, together with those as presents for the Great Council on hand here. I have applied to the local Militia and the U.S. Rangers for a guard, without effect. The public property in my hands remains unprotected. I have not even arms enough for the persons constituting my family. One rifle, a fowling piece, and an English musket are all I have to defend 30 or 40 thousand dollars worth of U.S. property. There is no calculating on the friendship of the Indians after the loss of Michelimackinac and Chicago. If Governor Hull is not strong enough to attack Malden, he never ought to have crossed over to the British territory.

I have the Honor to Remain with Very Great respect, Sir,
Your Most Obedient Servant,
John Johnston

"The Dilbone Massacre"

There are several accounts of the Dilbone Massacre. It occurred in 1813 on what is now State Route 36, east of Piqua. An account exists in every Miami County Ohio history book. The same can be said concerning a massacre involving Major Wolverton and some local soldiers. The first recorded accounts stem from the writings of Dr. Asa Coleman. Dr. Coleman was one of the county's first physicians, as well as a surgeon for the Ohio Militia during the War of 1812. His original version of these events was first published in 1837 by the Troy Times. Many of his recollections have been published, often not recognizing him as the primary source of information. This account holds information from all previous versions of the massacres, as well recently discovered letters from government and militia officials concerning the events.

The fears of Troy's citizens were later to be realized, but not by the Indians residing at the Johnston farm. Johnston was directed by the Federal Government to supply non-hostile Indians with a safe domain and supplies, and also to keep them congregated in some sort of orderly manner. Harrison sent many Indians to Johnston in order to keep promote neutrality. As the number of Indians increased, so did the tension in the county.

In mid August, 1813, a man named David Gerard was murdered by two Indians in a woods near his house. He had been making shingles with a man named Ross. After Gerard was shot, Ross escaped and ran to Staunton, where a company of volunteers were drilling, and warned the community. Men returned to the scene to find Gerard scalped. His family was unharmed. Two miles north, the same Indians came upon a man named Henry Dilbone and his family. Dilbone was shot through the chest, but ran into the cornfield and hid in order to escape. He saw the Indians tomahawk and scalp his wife, but was unable to come to her aid. He hid himself as well as he could, and was not found until the next day. He was still living when he was located by Captain Benjamin Dye. Dye and his men were returning from Fort Greenville. In his last minutes on this earth, Dilbone asked for his wife and children. Captain Dye told him his children were being cared for, and that his wife was dead. He asked to see her remains, and after looking at her, he fell back and died. John Dilbone, the eldest child, was seven years old. He witnessed the entire event. After seeing his parents killed, he took his two sisters and infant brother back to their home. The children put the infant to sleep, and all climbed into their parents bed. Later that day, a neighbor stopped in and asked they why they were in bed. John told her the horrid story. She immediately left for her children and the nearest station. Presently, William McKinney came, and John took him to the grizzly scene. John also mentioned that he knew the Indian who was responsible was a well known local, Mingo George. According to John, his mother had pleaded with her murderer when he had fired at her husband. "George, don't kill him", she begged. She was then tomahawked. McKinney took the children to Winan's Station for safety.

As for Mingo George, some time later he was killed by a well directed bullet while deer hunting along the Miami River. The local tribe he had been staying with buried him without comment. As a warrior, he had achieved one of his goals. The hostile Indians in the area wanted to drive wedges between the citizens and the Indians that Johnston was keeping at his farm. A goal that was not realized was that of taking Colonel Johnston's life. Johnston noted details of the attacks in a letter he penned the following letter to the National Intelligencer:

Piqua, Ohio August 21, 1813

On Wednesday evening the 18th of the present month, the British allies made an eruption into the neighborhood of Piqua. They fired on David Gerard and a Mr. Ross who had been working some distance from a house. Ross made his escape unhurt, but Gerard, not being able to get out of the way, fell sacrifice to the tomahawk and scalping knife. From this scene the savages proceeded some distance to where Henry Dilbone and his wife were pulling flax. They fired upon Dilbone and shot him through the body, after which they dispatched his wife with the knife and tomahawk, in the act of holding up her hands and begging for mercy. The murderous wretches made good their retreat and in all probability have returned to there employers at Malden to receive reward for their services.

Both Dilbone and Gerard have left families of small helpless children. The party who committed the above murders passed Wapaghkonetta where they were spoken to, avowed there intention of coming to Piqua, and said they were sent by the British. They also said several parties of Indians were sent to other parts of the frontier. From many circumstances which have come to my knowledge, I am induced to believe these visits will be repeated upon our defenseless inhabitants. Those residing in places of danger will do well to be on their guard.

In haste, Your Obedient Servant,
John Johnston

The frontier was a terribly dangerous place. Passing through the Miami Valley was equally difficult for red and white men. We know the fate of Mingo George. There is no record of disciplinary action against Major Wolverton or the men who attacked the peaceful Indians.... on the contrary, a neighboring county (Montgomery) history states that the Miami Militia was under orders to kill any Indians they encountered and take their squaws and children as prisoners. This story ends as it begins, with fear and panic on both sides, with settlers and Indians ready to kill.

MISCELLANY CONCERNING THE OHIO MILITIA

A review of several stand alone documents found in the following pages can help us understand Ohio Militia structure and Ohio's state of readiness at the outbreak of the war. Ohio became a state in 1803, and the northwestern part of the state remained sparsely settled. For example, in 1810, Dayton Ohio's population was approximately 385 people. Consequently local frontier militias were not fully staffed.

The Ohio Militia information in this publication also provides insight as to why General Harrison preferred using Kentucky Militia over the Ohio Militia...The Kentucky Militia was more experienced, better trained, better disciplined, and better equipped than Ohio's men.

The 1809 Constitution of the Dayton Rifle Company

Many Ohio Militia companies were equipped with muskets, but like most militia of the era, Ohio also employed rifle companies. The next few pages contain the 1809 Constitution of the Dayton Rifle Company. It provides insight to officers and their subordinates, uniform requirements, rules, regulations, fines for non-compliance, and the equipment a rifleman was expected to carry.

Constitution For the Dayton Rifle Company

August 17th 1809

We the undersigned do bind ourselves to support the following as the Constitution of said Company:

Section I
The Captain and Lieutenant shall appoint the non-commissioned officers.

Section II
A candidate for membership in this company must be recommended by two members and voted in by the members present ballot, and if two-thirds of the members then favor his admittance, he shall become a member by equipping himself according to the Constitution and signing the same.

Section III
After signing the Constitution, each member shall equip himself according to the same within six weeks after signing and all who do not uniform within the time aforesaid shall pay a fine of twenty-five cents for every Battalion and Regimental muster until they are completely uniformed.

Section IV
Deep blue hunting shirts, pantaloons with white fringes, bearskin over their hats, a white plume, a white vest, and white neckcloth shall be the complete uniform.

Section V
Six months after signing the Constitution, each member shall equip himself with a good rifle, shot pouch, powderhorn, tomahawk, and scalping knife.

Section VI
If an officer of said Company comes on parade not equipped according to the law, he shall for neglect pay a fine of fifty cents.

Section VII
Every member coming on parade not having his uniform and equipment in complete order shall pay a fine of twelve and one-half cents.

Section VIII
An officer of said Company behaving indecent when on parade shall pay a fine of one dollar.

Section IX
A person wishing to quit the Company, must have consent of a majority, or continue in the Company.

Section X
A member frequently misbehaving may be balloted out if two-thirds of the members of said Company then present vote against him.

Section XI
At the mind beat of the drum, or first calling of the role, any officer refusing to attend, or failing to be present, shall pay a fine of twenty-five cents. A private failing as aforesaid shall pay a fine of twelve and one half cents.

Section XII
The commanding officer of the day shall issue a warrant directed to any constable of the said township which warrants, or warrants shall be given to the orderly sergeant of said Company, who shall see that the same is collected, and he shall keep an account of money received and expended. He shall pay out none without a written order from the commanding officer.

Section XIII
Should the Captain transgress the laws, the Lieutenant who is highest in command shall issue a warrant against him accordingly as is pointed out in Section XII.

Section XIV
All fines and forfeitures shall be collected to section the twelfth and be appropriated to the use of Company as the officers may direct.

August 29, 1809

(Signed by)

Officers

William Vancleaf –Captain
Joseph Keamp –Lieutenant
William Hamen –Ensign
Lewis Davis –First Sergeant
John Enoch –Corporal

Muscians

John Jordun
Silas Rice
Daniel Stutsmen
Isaac Conover

John Baker
Mathew Thomson
Wm B. Guy
Adam Deam
John McClain
Thomas Reed
B. Tannott
B. Dilley
John Davis
James T. Snodgrass
Samuel Dille
John Kyle
John Wolf
John Bauker
Daniel Neff
Lewis Neff
James Willison
Jacob Houser
Joseph Maccron
Isaac Kemp

David Kemp
Philip Wagner
John Rench Jr.
Samuel Kemp
William Freybeck
John Burns
Henry Deam
Jacob M. Crain
Peter Fackel
Michael Heckman
Jonathon Mayhill
Abraham Neff
Tom Homer
Machal Radeback
Abraham Enoch
Daniel Flower
James B. Hill
Jacob Wilson
Peter Carter
James Brown

Matthew Thomson
Will Thomson
Josiah (X) Clawson
John Johnston
Phillip Wagner
James R. Guy
John Wert
D. Gabbry
James Johnson
Peter Carter
John Hanley
George Saylor
L.W. Reynold
Jacob Fockel
John Willson
Jacob Hettan
Abraham Capel
Peter Curtner
Frederick Hoover
Andreas Westfall

BASIC MILITIA STRUCTURE

Ohio Militia rank was:

Major General
Brigadier General
Colonel / Field Colonel
Lieutenant Colonel
Major
Captain
Lieutenant
Ensign
Sergeant
Corporal
Private

Division- Always commanded by a high ranking General

Brigade- Usually commanded by a Brigadier General

Regiment- Usually commanded by a Colonel

Battalion- Typically commanded by a Major

Company- Almost without exception commanded by a Captain, often with a Lieutenant as adjutant if it was a full company of about 100 men. There would always be one senior non-commissioned officer, the Company Sergeant (or First Sergeant). Depending on the size of the company, it may have a Sergeant and a Corporal.

Ohio Militia
1811 Muster Return

The 1811 Ohio Militia Muster Return sheds an accurate light on the Ohio Militia –in terms of their staffing, structure, and supply. There is a summary following the Muster Return. General Harrison probably used similar information when he planned his strategies. This Muster Return is an excellent tool for reenactors, researchers, and historians, as it is primary source information.

General Abstract for 1811-Ohio Militia Muster Return

# of Dvsn	Divisions — Major General & Division Staff			Brigades — Brig. General / Brig Staff			Regiments — Field Officers		Regiments — Regimental Staff									
	Major Generals	Quarter Master	Aids De Camp	Brigadier Genels	Brigade Majors	Brigade Q'Master	Colonels	Majors	Adjudents	Quarter Masters	Surgeons	Surgeons Mate	Clerks	Pay Masters	Sergeant Majors	Q'Master Sergeant	Drum Majors	Fife Majors
1st	1	1	2	5	5	5	13	28	17	17	15	14	17	16	16	14	15	14
2nd	1	1	2	4	4	4	12	25	13	13	11	8	14	14	13	13	11	12
3rd	1	1	2	4	4	4	14	28	12	13	13	9	13	13	12	12	9	11
4th	1	1	2	4	4	3	10	22	9	8	7	7	8	8	7	5	7	8
Totals	4	4	8	17	17	16	49	103	51	51	46	38	52	51	48	44	42	45

General Abstract for 1811-Ohio Militia Muster Return, continued

Battalion Return	Company Officers				Non-Commissioned Officers				Arms, Ammunition, and Accouterments									
	Major	Captain	Lieutenants	Ensigns	Sergeants	Corporals	Musicians	Rank & File	Swords & Belts	Spontoons	Muskets	Bayonets & Belts	Cartridge Boxes	Rifles	Pouches & Horns	Cartridges	Lbs. of Powder	Screws
1st		140	141	131	521	375	159	8670	249	89	1856		54	2501	2297		411	788
2nd		104	106	98	348	231	130	8731	153	53	916	55	28	2242	1274		30	416
3rd		107	105	108	573	234	104	5604	156	34	1261	22	10	1482	971	1500	121	322
4th		95	94	97	378	208	155	5282	152	53	894	136	206	1490	1131		14	210
Totals	451		446	444	1820	1038	575	25087	710	229	4927	213	298	7715	5673	1500	576	1731

General Abstract for 1811-Ohio Militia Muster Return, continued

| Comiss'd Officers | | total of men & Independent Rifle companies | Number of Men Including Officers | Number of Brigades | Number of Regiments | Fifes | Drums | Knapsacks | Stands of Colours | Screws | Flints | lbs of Lead | Loose Balls |
Lieutenants	Captains												
2	1	12000	10182	5	14	86	85	85	21	788	3791	1043	5357
2	1	7912	6928	4	12	78	73		33	416	2359	107	1006
		7937	7000	4	12	64	69		11	322	2691	76	625
		6877	6430	4	10	87	91	10	3	210	1704	2	653
Totals: 4	2	34726	30540	17	48	315	318	95	68	1731	11005	1228	7641

Arms, Ammunition, and Accouterments

27

General Abstract for 1811-Ohio Militia Muster Return, continued

	Iron Field Pieces						Brass Field Pieces						Non-Commisioned Officers					
	Total	3 Pounders	4 Pounders	6 Pounders	9 Pounders	12 Pounders	Total	3 Pounders	4 Pounders	6 Pounders	9 Pounders	12 Pounders	Matrosses	Musicians	Bombardiers	Gunners	Corporals	Sergeants
			1	4									25	2	3	3	2	2
													27	2	5	5		4
Totals			1	4									52	4	8	8	2	6

28

General Abstract for 1811-Ohio Militia Muster Return, continued

	# of Men & Officers	# of Companies	Fifes	Drums	Knapsacks	Wires & Brushes	Screws	Flints	Cartridges	Cartridge Boxes	Bayonets & Belts	Fusees	Swords & Belts	Small Arms Ammunition & Accouterments	Wagons	Trumbruls
	40	1	1	1				25		25	25	25	12			
	46	1	1	1									3			
Totals	86	2	2	2				25		25	25	25	15			

29

General Abstract for 1811-Ohio Militia Muster Return, continued

	Commissioned Officers			Non-Commissioned Officers				Cavalry — Arms, Ammunition, and Accouterments								
	Captains	Lieutenents	Coronets	Sergeants	Musicianers	Sadlers	Farriers	Rank & File	Pairs of Pistols	Pairs of Holsters	Cartridge Boxes	Cartridges	Horses	Saddles	Bridles	Breast Plates
	11	20	11	33	7	5	3	349	151	151	93	120	401	391	391	45
	5	10	5	9	3	5	4	152	60	60	32	140	193	193	193	67
	5	7	5	20	5	4	3	203	153	153	33	498	230	130	230	84
	2	3	2	8	1	1	1	63	25	21	13	162	72	72	72	15
Totals	23	40	23	70	16	15	11	767	389	385	171	920	896	886	886	211

30

General Abstract for 1811-Ohio Militia Muster Return, continued

Cavalry

Arms, Ammunition, and Accoutrements						Commissioned Officers			Non-Commis'd Officers			
Mail Pistols	Vaises	Stand of Colours	Swords	# of companies	# of Men and Officers	Captains	Lieutenants	Ensigns	Sergeants	Corporals	Musicians	Rank & File
31	5	5	165	11	443	2	2	2	6	6	4	67
67	40	3	56	5	193	1	1	1	4	4	2	64
100	0	2	140	5	252	4	4	4	12	7	6	127
19	20	1	24	2	81	2	2	2	6		2	78
217	**65**	**11**	**385**	**23**	**969**	**9**	**9**	**9**	**28**	**17**	**14**	**336**

Totals

General Abstract for 1811-Ohio Militia Muster Return, continued

Light Infantry

Arms, Ammunition, and Accouterments

# of Men & Officers	# of Companies	Fifes	Drums	Knapsacks	Stands of Colours	Wires & Brushes	Screws	Flints	Cartridges	Cartridge Boxes	Bayonets & Belts	Fusees	Espontoons	Swords & Belts
89	2	2	2		2	37	37	67		67	67	67	3	7
77	1	1	1		1		20	74	400	20	20	74	3	3
164	5	4	3				32	60		4		32	2	11
92	2	1	1		1			30				53	1	3
422	**10**	**8**	**7**		**4**	**37**	**89**	**231**	**400**	**91**	**87**	**226**	**9**	**24**

Totals

General Abstract for 1811-Ohio Militia Muster Return, concluded.

Riflemen — Arms, Ammunition, and Accouterments

# of Men & Officers		# of Companies	Bugle Horns	Knapsacks	Wires & Brushes	Flints	Screws	Loose Balls	lbs. of Lead	lbs. of Powder	Powder & Horns	Rifles	Espontoons	Swords & Belts
1246	21	3	72	162	1321	299	1922	304	148	1072	1072	14	39	
714	13	2	2	161	657	224	2529	83	74 1/4	454	449	13	22	
479	9	3		20	578	253	973	65	20	308	338	4	12	
274	5				30		300		23	7	172	2	8	
Totals 2709	48	8	74	343	2386	776	5726	452	265 1/4	1891	2031	33	81	

Notes:

183 men including Officers to be added in 2nd Brigade, 1st Division, the return of which came too late for Inspection.

One certain Regiment in the 4th Brigade, 3rd Division deficient for wanting the Collected Return.

Also, the 3rd Brigade, 3rd Division, supplied no return, but have fulfilled last years return.

I. Van Horn, Adjt General

1811 MUSTER RETURN SUMMARY

Within each Division's structure, it appears that the following existed:

Major General
Quarter Master General
2 Aides de Camp
4 or 5 Brigades, each having a
Brigadier General
Brigadier Major
Brigade QuarterMaster

Within each Brigade, there were 3 Regiments, each having a:

Regiment Colonel
2 Majors
1 Adjutant
1 Quarter Master
1 Surgeon
1 Surgeon's Mate
1 Clerk
1 Pay Master
1 Sergeant Major
1 Quarter Master Sergeant
1 Drum Major
1 Fife Major

BREAKDOWN BY DIVISION

1st Division
5 Brigades
14 Regiments
1 Artillery Company @ 40 men
11 Companies of Calvary @ 44 men each
2 Companies of Light Infantry @ 45 men each
21 Companies of Riflemen @ 59 men each

2nd Division
4 Brigades
12 Regiments
1 Artillery Company @ 46 men with four 6lb and one 4lb cannons
5 Companies of Calvary @ 39 men each
1 Company of Light Infantry @ 77 men each
13 Companies of Riflemen @ 55 men each

3rd Division
4 Brigades
10 Regiments
0 Artillery
2 Companies of Calvary @ 25 men each
5 Companies of Light Infantry @ 33 men each
9 Companies of Riflemen @ 56 men each

4th Division
4 Brigades
10 Regiments
0 Artillery
2 Companies of Calvary @ 40 men each
2 Companies of Light Infantry @ 46 men each
5 Companies of Riflemen @ 55 men each

It is interesting to note the variance of riflemen and their supplies, opposed to the ranks that were armed with muskets. Although Baron Von Steuben's revolutionary war drill became militia "law" in most states for several generations, it is obvious the weapons were not treated equally.

Counties and Militia Divisions

There are two lists given in most modern research concerning the Ohio Militia and Division structure during the War of 1812. Many authors cite only 4 divisions ...... as does the official State of Ohio Roster. At the advent of the War there were only 4 Divisions. In 1813, the state of Ohio organized 5 Divisions. Ohio was unprepared for war. The state drafted over 5000 men and the Militia had to reorganize to accommodate this increase. Greene and Miami Counties were exempt from draft. State officials assumed that if citizens would stay in these war-zone counties, they did so to protect their homes and property.

Researchers have not found much information concerning the Fifth Division because the documents and records kept by ranking officers such as regimental colonels were considered part of their personal property. Another reason for confusion in Division structure is that the 5th Divison's records may have been kept by the 1st Division. This is likely, as officers such as Holt, Munger, Price, and Whiteman are linked to the 5th Division —but there is also record of them serving in other Divisions within the Ohio Militia.

The 5th Division's function was to serve as companies on active duty under the state's domain, reinforce General Harrison's troops of US regulars, build and rebuild forts and blockhouses on the frontier, patrolling and scouting, and maintaining blockhouses.

The Daughters of the American Revolution state that it is possible that no documentation exists for up to one third of the men who served during the War of 1812. Poor record keeping also caused men to receive less or sometimes no bounty land for their service. (Bounty land claims will be discussed later in this book.)

The next few pages show both Division structures. The Fifth Division's tasks are outlined in the letters that follow militia structure. This is revealed in letters to Ohio's Governor Meigs, from General Whiteman and General Wingate.

Ohio Militia 1812 - 4 Divisons

First Division

First Brigade
Hamilton
Clermont

Second Brigade
Warren

Third Brigade
Butler

Fourth Brigade
Greene
Champaign

Fifth Brigade
Montgomery
Miami
Preble
Darke

Second Division

First Brigade
Adams
Highland

Second Brigade
Ross
Scioto

Third Brigade
Fayette

Fourth Brigade
Franklin
Delaware
Madison
Knox
Pickaway
Richland

Third Division

First Brigade
Washington
Adams
Gallia

Second Brigade
Fairfield
Licking

Third Brigade
Belmont

Fourth Brigade
Muskingum
Tuscarawas

Fourth Division

First Brigade
Jefferson

Second Brigade
Columbiana
Wayne
Stark

Third Brigade
Trumbell
Portage
Cuyahoga

Fourth Brigade
Guauga
Ashtabula

Ohio Militia 1813 - 5 Divisons

First Division

First Brigade
Hamilton
Clermont

Second Brigade
Warren
Clinton

Third Brigade
Butler

Second Division

First Brigade
Adams
Highland

Second & Third
Brigade
Ross
Scioto
Fayette

Fourth Brigade
Franklin
Delaware
Madison

Fifth Brigade
Pickaway

Third Division

First Brigade
Washington
Adams
Gallia

Second Brigade
Fairfield
Licking
Knox
Richland

Third Brigade
Belmont
Seventh Range of
Guernsey

Fourth Brigade
Muskingum
Coshocton
West of the seventh
range of Guernsey

Fourth Division

First Brigade
Jefferson
Harrison

Second Brigade
Columbiana

Wayne
Stark

Third Brigade
Trumbell

Fourth Brigade
Guauga
Portage
Ashtabula
Medina
Huron
Cuyahoga

Fifth Division

First Brigade
Greene
Champaign

Second Brigade
Montgomery
Preble
Miami
Darke

BENJAMIN WHITEMAN TO MEIGS
Falls Little Miami August 22d. 1813

His Excellency
Return J. Meigs
Dr. Sir

Your order of the 19th Inst by Mr. Vance I received last evening which I have now before me -- By an order from General Harrison to me through General McArthur I ordered a company sometime in May from this Division to Fort McArthur, where they yet remain under the command of Captain McClelland, I suppose there is at this time 60 effective men at that post, of this, I presume you and General Harrison must be apprised-- you state that General Harrison has requested and you wish me to send one full company to McArthurs "from this I suppose you deem it important that an additional company should be stationed at that post -- this order I shall proceed to execute so soon as it is in my power, but in the present state of things it is utterly impossible owing to the scarcity of private arms and ammunition in this quarter and a total want of public -- until lately there has been deposited at Urbana arms & ammunition with which the militia has been supplied when called into actual services. Recently they have been removed and upon inquiry of the Quarter Master at that place some three or four days past I was informed that there was neither arms nor ammunition fit for service - independent of the company stationed at McArthurs I have ordered a company to the head of Lost Creek there to build a Block House, another company I have ordered to rendezvous at Urbana and then to be divided upon (?) to be stationed at McPhersons and the residue to Zanesville -- I have moreover had diverse companies scouting on the frontiers -- the companies now ordered out I know not how they will be supplied with arms and ammunition, but do suppose that many will be compelled to be discharged for want of them. I am confident there is not more than one fourth of the Militia in this Division armed -- Mr. Vance informs me in a letter to me upon his return, that you observed, that "there was no necessity of giving me any further instructions about supporting the frontiers, as this Division is set apart for that purpose" if this is the fact I have not before understood it, for we have always furnished our proportion of every draft from the commencement of hostilities -- the calls upon this division for frontier duty and general duty upon state calls has been really burdensome upon the people, especially which we taken into view the irregularity of many requisitions, so much so that the individuals get neither credit for duty performed or pay for actual service -- My powers as it respects calling out the militia I conceive to be limited, in cases of urgent necessity I consider myself authorized to order out the militia until they can be regularly called upon --but whenever they can be regularly called upon by an order emanating from the commander in Chief of the State, I think it most proper for it so to be done - your ideas upon this subject I should be glad to receive and how far they are entitled to pay when thus ordered out by a militia officer.

Our frontier is at present in considerable alarm, arising from the murders recently committed, and I believe by some who pretend to wear the face of friendship - Two men by the name of Thomas on the night of the 12th. were killed at Solomon's Town -- on Friday a party went out to bring them in, and on their return between where the men were killed and McPhersons, they met with a party of Indians of those professing friendship, the Indians as soon as they saw them raised the war hoof and in other respects acted as if an attack was intended, they were fired upon by one of our men and with much a do our men were restrained from destroying them all - the Indians acted in a manner, indicating exultation or defiance as I am informed - a few days since as I am informed a man by the name of Gurtridge being out on a scout came across an Indian lying asleep with three rifles by him, two of those it is conjectured belonged to the Thomas's whether this is a fact or not, has not as yet been ascertained the Indian: and guns were brought in -- On the 18th in the evening a man was shot by an Indian near the head of lost Creek and a woman tomhawked -- the man ran and was pursued by the Indian --the Indian at length fell, and upon my (?) returned to the woman without his gun, left the children that were with their parents in the flax patch and went off -- the man lay near them that night the next day he was found, the Indians gun was also found -- A Mr. Keizer upon seeing the gun -- after it was found stated that he would swear that he shot at a mark in Washington with an Indian who shot with that gun, the gun is rather a remarkable one and can easily be recognized after having been once seen -- about the same time of the same day another man was killed about three miles off -- On the 11th a woman was shot in the arm by an Indian six miles west of

Springfield -- Those are the injuries which have been done on our frontiers so far as I have been informed -- I am well assured that unless the Indians are removed from our frontiers that the people will rise en masse and remove them, if they cannot by gentle method by force, for I do assure you so long as they remain on the frontier it is impossible to guard against mischief -- we know not a hostile Indian until too late -- I was last evening informed by Mr. Wilson that there was a party of about 1000 men out with the determination of bringing the Indians in and to kill all who would not consent to come in --You may rest assured sir that every thing in my power to protect the frontier shall be done, I should be happy to receive your answer by the first opportunity.

With every sentiment of respect believe me to remain your very Humble Servant.

> *Benjamin Whiteman*
> *Major General Commanding. 5th Division Ohio Militia*

The next letter provides additional detail concerning the Fifth Division's activities on the frontier ....

Hamilton the 12th of Nov 1813

Governor Meigs,

Sir you will no doubt recollect of authorizing me about sixteen months ago to order out a company of Militia from the Brigade under my command for the protection of the frontier settlements. I did so and they have not yet received and compensation for their services so rendered, etc.

Likewise Mr. Thomas Blair who furnished the detachments with provision etc, stands in the same situation the vouchers were forwarded for the consideration of the legislator the last Session as the proper source some time has elapsed and no arrangements made for the defraying the expenses of said detachment and I am well convinced that your interposition will prevent further delay therefore flatter myself you will indulge those concerned with your attention to the premises aforesaid, Likewise Major Price who commanded a Battalion of Militia detach from the Brigade commanded by General Munger of the Fifth Division of Ohio Militia and stationed at Greenville Fort Nesbit and Brown. The commanding Major reported them to me while I commanded at St. Mary's as being in the service of the United States and after examining his different orders and finding this was their purport and corresponding with the letters I had received from General Monger relative, I reported them to General Harrison in my general return as attached to the second Regiment of the third detachment of Militia ordered from State of Ohio requiring his sanction provided it was a legal measure, and if not such instructions as he thought expedient or proper, the General thought the subject unworthy of his attention although four hundred of the troops under his direction was concerned, the Battalion have served six months faithfully and want a compensation for their services so rendered. I wrote to Mr. Curt (?) district paymaster relative, he gives me to understand that the troops must be mustered by a united states officers which I considered as illegal and further stated that I must give him assurances that they were ordered out by authority of the United States before he would make any arrangements to pay them and this was beyond my reach which leaves him without resource unless through the in (?) of your Excellency which I trust will not be neglected as their necessities render it important to them, a certificate to the district pay master from your Excellency purporting that said battalion was ordered out by authority of the United States if this was the case, would enable them to draw their pay their times of service generally expired in August but some later, I would be glad to hear from you on the subject as soon as possible. If I may ask such indulgence.

I am with the Highest Esteem and Consideration Sir,
Your very Humble Servant.

John Wingate
Brigadier. General.
Late commanding 3d Detachment. of Ohio Militia

.......and to further complicate matters, when one reviews the signatures on the next two letters, it appears that the Fourth Division took a Sixth Division under it's wing ...... in a manner similar to the way the First Divison formed the Fifth Division.....

WADSWORTH TO MEIGS
Headquarters 1st. August 1812

Sir,

Since writing the accompanying letter I have received a letter from General Beall, informing me that he shall march his troops into Wayne and Richland Counties which is contrary to express orders I have given him, He further mentions that he and several other officers have solicited You to approve of his conduct. I trust Sir Your Excellency will not intentionally establish a precedent which will at once destroy all subordination in the Militia.

Very respectfully I remain Your Obedient Servant,

Elijah Wadsworth Major General.
6th Division

WADSWORTH TO MEIGS

Cleveland August 25th 1812

Sir,

In consequence of the surrender of Detroit which has left the whole of this part of the frontier defenseless. I have ordered the second, third, fourth, and a

part of the first brigades - under my command to rendezvous at this place. A part of the men have already arrived and the others are on the march -- Mr. Huntington starts this morning for the City of Washington to make application to the Secretary at War for Arms ammunition etc, to enable me the more effectually to protect the property and lives of the Inhabitants -- I hope Sir that the disposition of these troops at this critical period will be satisfactory to the Commander in Chief and the Government of the United States --

> *Elijah Wadsworth Major General.*
> *4th Division*

Return J. Meigs Esquire
Governor of the State of Ohio

It appears that the Ohio Militia's structure changed rapidly as drafted men and volunteers entered into service. It is small wonder that recordkeeping was an issue. To further complicate things, state militias answered to the state governor. Ohio's Governor, R.J. Meigs, (who incidentally was General Hull's brother-in-law) made himself known in person on the frontier and personally dispatched and reassigned men. It is likely he did so to respond to immediate needs, as by position, he was privy to information before others, and he did not have the luxury of a cell phone or email.... The Ohio Militia's hierarchy found this terribly frustrating, as by personally dispatching men, he bypassed the chain of command. This is evident in the following letter from Major General John Gano to Major Thomas Van Horne.....

Dear Sir,

I expected to have had the pleasure of seeing you before this, which prevented or was the cause of not answering your acceptable letter before this. I am glad you are one of the committee appointed to revise the Militia Law, it certainly is very deficient in many parts. I requested several officers that I considered most competent to make their observations and send them forward which I presume has been done. The mode of ordering Militia on duty on the frontier has caused much complaints as you will see by the enclosed copy of a letter received from General Whiteman and General Munger complains there is and has been so many of his Brigade on duty, that he has not been able to get a return of the Brigade to forward to me. The Governor ordering detachments in small detailed portions without any return to the Major, Colonel, or Commander of the Brigade, puts it out of the officers power whose duty it is to do a justice to his command as he does not and cannot know who is on duty or who has performed their tour, and throws the whole (system) into confusion; a Militia office is truly an arduous, troublesome, expensive, and unthankful one, if strictly and properly attended to. I have wrote to Governor Meigs, suggesting the propriety of the upper brigades being struck into a Division, and the lower 3 brigades will form a Compact Division, and be then better disciplined and attended to, and may then have assistance to regulate and bring some kind of order to the BULLWORK OF THE COUNTRY.

My poor little Mary has broke her arm very badly, and I am in haste.

Your friend and Humble Servant

John S. Gano

Take note.......... Governor Meigs is legally ordering out small detachments, but not through the chain of command. The confusion created by the influx of men is then compounded. It is no wonder that many people that served in frontier Ohio had difficulty obtaining bounty land. There was no way to track their movement or their tours of duty.... Something else that is not often seen in militia structure is also occurring...........Proposals to organize men into Divisions based on their current geographic location rather than by their home counties.

FLINTLOCK PHRASES

You might not have grown up using these phrases, but chances are that grandparents did ....

<u>Lock, Stock, and Barrel</u> –Muskets and rifles were traded by component, or complete.

<u>Go Off Half Cocked</u> –Taking action before fully readied . Flintlocks sometimes malfunction in this manner ..... usually while loading, and the result can be disastrous.

<u>Flash In The Pan</u> –Off to a good start, but no action following.

<u>Hang Fire</u> –A malfunction where all the basics were in place and executed, yet with no end result.

-Another interesting phrase that is still used is **"<u>Bite the Bullet</u>"**. It means to tough out a situation. At many archeological sites, digs reveal lead balls that have been chewed. The reason for this is that lead contains arsenic, which in small amounts is a pain killer. Soldiers chewed on lead balls to deal with unresolved dental issues.....

OBTAINING BOUNTY LANDS

The following bounty land documents are from two men who served as Rangers/Riflemen on the frontier. As mentioned in previous text, we discussed many soldiers records of service are/were missing. While it is generally true that the higher one's rank, the more likely that records exist, but most soldiers were not officers. The DAR has suggested that there is no documentation for up to a third of the men who served in this war.

Officers kept their unit's papers as personal property, the state's governor ordered detachments out while ignoring militia hierarchy, Divisions were formed and disbanded within a year, and one Division might be the recordkeeper for another.

It was difficult for many men to prove their tours of duty forty years after the fact. Some were able to obtain the lands they were rightfully due, but many were unable.

Ohio Militia records from the War of 1812 are periodically found –some have been discovered in the last twenty years. In accordance with state law, Ohio Militia records are public domain. By publishing them as they are discovered, we will hve a more complete understanding of Ohio's role in the War of 1812.

THE BOUNTY LAND WARRANT PAPERS FOR MAJOR JACOB MANN

An Explanation of Pages 50-60

Paqe 50 is Major Mann's initial application for a land pension, and details his service on the frontier. It is dated September 21, 1850

Page 51 shows sworn affidavits by men that knew Jacob Mann, along with notes that show the application was in process.

Page 52 shows that the pension office cannot identify Jacob as having served as a Major, but do have record of him serving as a Captain.

Page 53 relays the pension office's findings and is notification that his service record is incomplete.

Page 54 is a request for the pension office to perform further investigation.

Page X5 shows that his service was finally credited, and he was eventually granted 160 acres. The document is dated May 18, 1851.

Page 56-60 outline Jacob Mann's military record. Had the comments on page 60 not been recorded thirty-seven years earlier, there would be not have been any record of his service as an Major for the Ohio Militia. It was the only record in existence.

State of Ohio

Montgomery County ss On this twenty first day of September One
thousand Eight hundred and fifty. Personaly appeared
before me a Justice of the Peace. for the County and State aforesaid
Jacob Mann, Who being duly Sworn according to law on his Oath
Saith. That he is the Identical Jacob Mann. Who was Captain
of a Company Volunteers that was raised in Miami County. And was
ordered on a tour of duty on the frontier with said Company, in the
early part of said year, by Col. John Mann, Who Commanded the 1st Reg.
2nd Brigade 3rd Division Ohio Militia; That he served out said tour
of Duty. And on his returned That he served as expressed in
the discharge Annexed. and that he is the Identical Jacob Mann
therein named, and that he served as Ensign to said Company.
And he further Saith that Some time in October in the same year
he was drafted from the Regt. Brigade & Division above mentioned
in the Six Months drafted Militia. And that he Served the first
Part of Said teem as a Captain, and the latter part as Major
of the Said Reg. and That a Short teem previous to the expiration
of his Said teem he was Ordered home, to assist in making
a new Draft. And that he has served more the Six months
in the War with Great Britian. Exclusive of the time mentioned
in the annexed discharge. That he never received any other
discharge but the one annexed. That he has never received a bounty
land for Said Service or any other Service, or authorized any person
or persons to do So for him

Sworn & Subscribed to before me   Jacob Mann
this Day & year above written
John Andrew J.P.

The State of Ohio,
Montgomery County, as Before me John Anderson a
Justice of the Peace in and for said County personally came
Henry Mann and William Geisman, two creditable witnesses,
who being duly sworn according to law deposith and saith
they are well acquainted with Jacob Mann and
know him to be the Identical Jacob Mann who served
in the War of Eighteen hundred and twelve of thirteen in
the Offices he states in the foregoing affadavit — And
that they are disinterested in his said application, con-
tained in the same for Bounty Land. Henry Mann
Sworn & Subscribed to before   William Geisman
me this 21st day of September 1850
            John Anderson J.P.

Sir   Dayton O. Sepr 21st 1850
        I have the honor of forwarding my Claim for
Bounty Land. You will please Examine the same
and if found intitled you will forward my Certificate
to John Anderson J.P. who is my true and lawful attorney
in the premises
Witness   Respectfully
J. T. Remy   your Obt Servt.
William Chartel

                                Jacob Mann

J. L. Edwards, Esqr
    Commissioner of Pensions

                    Dayton O. Sepr 21st 1850
Sir   I herewith forward you Mr Jacob Mann's
    application for Bounty Land Please Examine
    the same & forward the result to me at this
    place
                    Very Respectfully
                            your Obt Servt.
To J. L. Edwards Esqr   John Anderson
    Commissioner of Pensions
            Pension Office
                Washington City

51

THIRD AUDITOR'S OFFICE,

December 24 1850

It appears from documents on file in this Office, that _Jacob Manns_ a of Captain of a Company of Ohio Militia, entered the service on the 14th November, 1812 and served till the 14th March 1813

Jno. S. Gallaher
Auditor

No 95

Treasury Department
3 Auditors Office
May 7 57

The files in this office does not afford
any evidence of the service of Jacob
Mann as Major of Ohio Militia

B. F. Callahen
For B Auditor

Pension Office
Jany. 22d 1852.

Sir

The papers in the application of Jacob
Mann for bounty land, are respectfully referred to
your office again, to see if said Mann has performed
any other service beside the one mentioned in your certificate— You will perceive that he claims to have performed other tours of duty beside the one mentioned—

Very Respectfully
Yr. Obt. Servt.
F. S. Evans
for Commissioner

Jno. S. Gallaher Esq.
3d Auditor
Treasy. Dept.

54

No 95 def 27/53

Jacob Mann bef Ng

1st Reg 5 Brigade

5th Division Ohio Militia

ab ar 1812

3d Aud. Oct off,, Land

Suspended in let.
to 3. Aud Aug 22/57

Allowed 160 acres

Warrant No 385 issued
and sent 18th May 1857

John Anderson
Dayton Ohio

vol 63 Pay 55

352

Mann, Jacob

Adams' Batt'n (1812-13), Ohio Militia.
(War of 1812.)

Captain Captain

CARD NUMBERS.

1	3777 4017	22	
2	4064	23	
3		24	
4		25	
5		26	
6		27	
7		28	
8		29	
9		30	
10		31	
11		32	
12		33	
13		34	
14		35	
15		36	
16		37	
17		38	
18		39	
19		40	
20		41	
21		42	

Number of personal papers herein 2

Book Mark: _____

See also _____

W

Jacob Man

Capt , Capt. Adams Batt~ Co.

Ohio Militia Reg't

L Inclosures.

(War of 1812.)

Pay accounts	1	Final Statements
Subsistence accounts	1	Furloughs or L. of A
Certs. of Dis. for Discharge		Med. Certificates
C. M. Charges		Med. Des. Lists
Descriptive Lists		Orders
Discharge Certificates		Pris. of War Record
Pension Warrant		Resignations

Other papers relating to—

Admission to Hosp'l	Furlough or L. of A
Casualty Sheet	Med. Examination
Confinement	Misc. Information
Contracts	Pay or Clothing
Death or Effects	Personal Reports
Desertion	Rank
Discharge from Hosp'l	Transfer to Hosp'l
Discharge from Service	Transfer to V. R. C.
Duty	Transportation

NAMES	RANK	Commencement of pay as per pay-roll	Ending of pay	Time paid for (months)	Time paid for (days)	Pay per month (dolls)	Pay per month (cents)	Amount receivable (dolls)	Amount receivable (cents)	SIGNERS' NAMES	WITNESSES	REMARKS
Jacob Manor	Capt	_____	_____	4		60		40	00	Jacob Manor	_____	

58

Subsistence Account of Capt Jacob Mann of _____ detatchment of men from the said Regiment on _____ _____ by Edmund Munger _____ Genl _____ ordered _____ _____ the 11th Nov 1813 _____ _____ Fort _____ at Greenville

	Commencement	Expiration	No of Days Subsistence	No of Rations Pr day	Total No of Rations	State of settlement		Remarks
						Ration at 8cts	
	12th July 1813	20 March 1813	68	2	136	2 cents	97	10

I certify on honor, that the foregoing account is accurate and Just, and that I have not drawn the rations on hand from the United States, or received money on said thereof, or ordered any part of the time above charged — — — — — — —

_____ _____ _____ that Old Payments Twenty Seven Dollars and twenty cents being my substitution in full from the 12 day of July 1813 to the 20th March 1813 inclusive having Signed duplicate _____

Jacob Mann Capt

Jacob Mann Capt

Left form (Pay Roll):

𝒥ℳ | Adams' Battalion. (1812-13) | **Ohio Militia.**

Jacob Mann

Appears with the rank of *Capt.* .... on a

Pay Roll

of a Company of Ohio Militia commanded by Capt. Jacob Mann, and a part of the time by Ensign John Knight, of Major G. Adams' Batt'n,*

(War of 1812,)

for *Mar. 14, 1812 to May 13,* 1813 .

Roll dated ......*Not dated*...., 181 .

Commencement of service } *Nov. 14....*, 1812 . or of this settlement,

Expiration of service or } *Mch. 14.*, 1813 . of this settlement,

Term of service charged, ... months, ... days.

Pay per month, ... dollars, ... cents.

Amount of pay, ... dollars, ... cents.

Remarks: ....

....

....

*This company was designated at various times as Captain Jacob Mann's and Ensign John Knight's Company.

.....*Burnham*.....

(672e) Copyist.

Right form (Muster Roll):

𝒥ℳ | Adams' Battalion. (1812-13) | **Ohio Militia.**

Jacob Mann

Appears with the rank of *Capt.* .... on a

Muster Roll

of a detachment of Drafted Militia commanded by Capt. Jacob Mann, Major G. Adams' Batt'n, Ohio Militia,*

(War of 1812,)

for *Mar. 14, 1812 to March 14,* 1813 .

Roll dated ......*Not dated*...., 181 .

Commencement of service, *Nov. 14....*, 1812 .

Expiration of service, *Mch. 14.*, 1813 .

Present or absent, *Present.*

Remarks: *It will be remembered that at the expiration of the term herein expressed I was Eligible Major. I was relieved by Col. John Mason Com'd't of the 2d Regiment 5 Brigade 2d Division Ohio Militia to the command of highest Battalion of said Regiment but to give up the command of the detachment to Ensign John Knight.*

Jacob Mann, Capt.

*This company was designated at various times as Captain Jacob Mann's and Ensign John Knight's Company.

.....*Burnham*.....

(560e) Copyist.

THE BOUNTY LAND WARRANT PAPERS FOR PRIVATE ISAAC MANN

An Explanation of Pages 62-67

Page 62 is a letter to Private Isaac Mann suspending his claim for a land pension, pending proof of his service on the frontier. It is dated February 26, 1852.

Page 63 shows the pension office has granted him 40 acres.

Page 64 is Isaac Mann's pension application and details of his service.

Page 65 relays the pension office's findings and a forwarded statement to Isaac Mann and his attorney.

Page 66 is a pension packet cover letter.

Page 67 shows the final determination of his application and conformation of a 120 acre grant. It appears he was able to prove additional service, but the packet is unfortunately incomplete.

Piqua Feb 26. 1852

Sir

The Claim of Isaac Mann referred to in the Circular ~~Nineteenth~~ has been Suspended for proof of longer Service.

It will not be possible for Mr Mann to obtain the proof required So that you may issue for the Amount that Appears to be due from the Auditors reports.

It is probable that Mr Mann is in an Error in regard to the term he actually did Serve.

I Am Sir

Respt Yours,
N. F. Wilbur

J. E. Heath
Comr of Pensions

99 025 Sep 17/51

65.237 Isaac Mann

Private & Mul
Capt Williams
Col. Mann

War 1812   18 Oct 12
Sm   Aug 25, 1812
Dis Feb 1813

3 Audt office
Jan 28 1852

Isaac Mann served
under Capt Williams
from 23 August to the
26 October 1812

B. H. Gaeske

H. Baud
A 40 acres mch 7/12
W 46.353 of A.Va.
March 7/12
M. F. Wilber
VR 2 P 174
Piqua
Ohio
L 0 7 26 Oct 1812

STATE OF OHIO, } 88.
Miami COUNTY. On this 11*th* day of *April*
A. D., 185*1*, personally appeared before me *A Notary Public* within
and for the County and State aforesaid *Isaac Mann* aged
fifty-nine years, a resident of the County of *Shelby* in the State of
Ohio who, being duly sworn according to Law, declares that he is the identical
Isaac Mann who was a *Private* in the Company com-
manded by Captain *John Williams* in the Regiment of *Ohio Militia*
commanded by *Col. Mann in the War with Great Brittain declared by the
U. States on the 18th day of June 1812* That he *Volunteered* at
Miami Co. Ohio on or about the *August* day of A. D. 18*12*,
for the term of *Six months* and continued in actual service in said War for the term of
Six Months and was honorably discharged at *Miami Co Ohio*
on or about the *February* day of *March* A. D. 18*13, as will appear
by a the Muster Rolls of said Company, that he never received
a written discharge.*

    That he makes this declaration for the purpose of obtaining the
Bounty land to which he may be entitled under the "Act granting Bounty Lands to certain officers and
soldiers, who have been engaged in the military service of the United States," Passed September 28, 1850.

              Isaac his Mann
                     x
                    mark

    SWORN TO AND SUBSCRIBED before me the day and year above written. And I
hereby certify that I believe the said *Isaac Mann* to be the
identical man who performed the military service aforesaid and to be of the age above stated.

                    N. F. Wilbur
                        Notary Public.

Piqua, *Ohio April* 11*th* 185*1*.

Sir :
    We herewith present the claim of *Isaac Mann* for
Bounty Land under the Act of Congress, passed September 28, 1850, entitled "An Act granting Boun-
ty Land to certain Officers and Soldiers who have been engaged in the military service of the United
States." We are Sir, Respectfully yours,

                    YOUNG & WILBUR.
                        N. F. Wilbur 99

To J. L. EDWARDS,
        Commissioner of Pensions.

64

(No. 2.)

SIR:

The application of *Isaac Maun*

for Bounty Land under act of 28th September, 1850, filed by you, has been examined and suspended. He claims service in Captain *Williams'*

company of *Ohio Mil.* sufficient to entitle him to *80*

acres. The Auditor reports that the rolls show that he served *from 23ᵈ Aug. to 26ᵗʰ Oct. 1812*

a period that would only entitle him to *40* acres. Before a warrant for a greater amount can issue, it is necessary, in the absence of an authentic discharge, that his service be established by the positive testimony of at least *two* officers or soldiers with whom he served, and whose names may be found on the rolls, or who have obtained warrants for like service. In the latter case the number and amount of each warrant must be given.

Very respectfully,

J. E. HEATH,
Commissioner.

N. F. Wilbur Esq,

Piqua

Ohio

Piqua Apr 7th 1855

Sir
    Enclosed I present to you the Claims of Isaac
Mann for Bounty Land under act of March 3d 1855
                                    I am Sir
S. P. Waldo   Respd, Yours
Court of Pensions   N. F. Wilber

66

3—247.

No. 65.237
99.028

ACT OF _Mar. 3_, 18 55

Received _____, 18___

Isac Mann
Pvt

Capt. John Williams

Wag. Mann

Ohio Mil.
War, 1812

Warrant No. 31.626

For 120 acres.

LIBERTY HALL
CINCINNATI
TUESDAY - JUNE 30, 1812

ORDER OF MARCH OF

ARMY OF OHIO
COMMANDED BY BRIGADIER GENERAL HULL

Spies

0 · 0   0   0   0   0   0

Van-guard

(diagram of Order of March — columns of troops labeled: Cavalry, Gen Hull and suite, Cavalry; Band of Music; Part of U.S. 4th Regt; Flank guard of Riflemen; Part of Cass's Regt; Part of Findlay's Regt)

Rear-guard

EXTRACT—FROM THE ARMY—DATED
"SOLOMONS TOWN, JUNE 18, 1812

"Hitherto affairs have gone on smoothly. An attempt was made at mutiny, by one company, who refused to march from Urbana.... But a few of the Tippecanoe boys being drawn up to fire upon them, they upon changed their tone. The leaders were apprehended...convicted, and brought forward for punishment.....but on due submission and entreation, they were pardoned."

ANOTHER ABSTRACT—DATED
"CAMP AT FORT M'ARTHUR, 40 MILES FROM URBANA, "JUNE 21, 1812

"We have had grand times since we left Urbana—rain every day, and mud ankle deep in our very tents— The army now consists of 2100 men—a regiment goes ahead by turns to open the road and erect a blockhouse at every twenty miles. We shall leave this place to-morrow morning."

M'Arthurs Regiment are in advance, for the purpose of opening roads and erecting blockhouses, and 900 men are to be added to the column in a few days....

By the President of the United States of America,

A PROCCLAMATION.

WHEREAS th Congress of The United States virtue of the constituted authority vested in them, have declared by their act, bearing the date the 18th day of the present month, that

WAR EXISTS

Between the United Kingdom of Great Britain and Ireland, and the dependencies thereof, and the United States of America and their territories: Now therefore I, James Madison, President of the same U. States of America, do hereby proclaim the same to all whom it may concern: and I do especially enjion on all persons holding offices, civil or military, under the authority of the United States, that they be vigilant and zealous in discharging duties respectively incident thereto. And I do moreover exhort all the good people of the United States, as they love their country, as they value the precious heritage derived from the virtue and valor of their fathers, as they feel the wrongs which have forced on them the last resort of injured nations, and as they consult the best means, under the blessing of Divine Providence, of bridging its calamities—that they exert themselves in preserving order in promoting concord, in maintaining the the authority and the efficacy of the laws, and in supporting and envigorating all the measures which may be adopted by the constituted authorities for obtaining a speedy, a just, and an honorable peace.

In testimony whereof I have hereunto set my hand, and caused the seal of the U. States to be affixed to these presents,
(seal)
Done at the city of Washington, the 19th day of June 1812, and the independence of the United States, the 36th.

signed James Madison   James Monroe
President   Secr'y of State

WAR!

THE DIE IS CAST— WAR IS DECLARED.

The long suffering forebearance of our government has ben completely worn out. The public mind has been for some time in a state of the most anxious suspence; and it is believed that this decisive measure, tho long delayed, is most welcome to a great majority of the people of this state, as well as of the United States. After this, let tories and traitors beware.

By last night's mail we recieved letters from Gen Worthington and Mr. Morrow, announcing the war—and also the National Intelligencer, containing the president's message to congress, detailing the outrages we have so long suffered from England, and recommended to their early deliberation "whether the United States will continue passive under these progressive and accumulating wrongs; or opposing force to force, commit a just cause into the hands of the Almighty Deposer of events." The committee of Foreign Relations, at the close of a long report, state that reiving on the the patriotism of the nation, and confidently trusting that the Lord of Hosts will go with us to battle in a righteous cause, and crown our efforts with success—your committee recommended an immediate appeal to ARMS.

Fourth Of July

A meeting of the citizens of Cincinnati was held last evening, at the Court house, and a committee appointed to make arrangements for the celebration of the approaching anniversary of AMERICAN INDEPENDENCE.

Town Lots

On the 25th of August next, will be offered for sale, on the spot, to the highest bidders, the IN and OUT LOTS of the TOWN of

Ludlow,

situate at the well known Medical watering place, the YELLOW SPRINGS, in Greene County. The sit of this place is dry, elevated and elegant. The air and water are

SOME SITES OF SIGIFICANCE IN OHIO DURING

THE WAR OF 1812

SITE	CURRENT LOCATION
Buchanon's Blockhouse	Miami County
Chillicothe	Ross County
Cleveland	Cuyahoga County
Dayton	Montgomery County
Dye's Blockhouse	Miami County
Fort Loramie	Shelby County
Fort Amanda	Auglaize County
Fort Ball	Seneca County
Fort Barbee	Auglaize County
Fort Black	Darke County
Fort Brier	Darke County
Fort Feree	Paulding County
Fort Findlay	Handcock County
Fort Greenville	Darke County
Fort Jennings	Putman County
Fort McArthur	Hardin County
Fort Meigs	Wood County
Fort Miami	Lucas County
Fort Morrow	Delaware County
Fort Nesbit	Darke County
Fort Piqua	Miami County
Fort Seneca	Seneca County
Fort Winchester	Defiance County
Franklinton	Franklin County
Hilliard's Blockhouse	Miami County
Hunter's Blockhouse	Miami County
Huron	Erie County
Jackson's Blockhouse	Shelby County

Johnston's Farm	Miami County
Manary's Blockhouse	Logan County
Mansfield Blockhouse	Richland County
Marietta	Washington County
New Lisbon	Columbiana County
Noftsinger's Blockhouse	Darke County
Piqua	Miami County
Portage Blockhouse	Wood County
Roger's Blockhouse	Miami County
Simmon's Blockhouse	Miami County
Staunton	Miami County
Steubenville	Jefferson County
Studebaker's Blockhouse	Darke County
Thomas' Blockhouse	Miami County
Urbana	Champaign County
Williams' Blockhouse	Miami County
Wooster	Wayne County
Zanesville	Muskingum County

Miami County Officers

These frontiersmen served as Riflemen, Rangers, and in volunteer companies .... in a county that was exempt from initial draft because it was considered warzone .... Many got their land in the Miamis from previous service, and they and assumed this service meant bounty lands later....

William Barbee Sr.- Captain
Richard Benham-Corporal
Barnabas Blue-Corporal
James Blue-Lieutenant
Garner Bobo-Lieutenant
William Brown-Corporal
George Buchanan-Captain
James Caldwell-Lieutenant
Joseph Coleman-Captain
Benjamin Dye-Captain
John Dye-Corporal
Vincent Dye-Sergeant
Alexander Ewing- Colonel
Elias Gerard-Corporal
Nathaniel Gerard-Corporal
Thomas Gilbert-Sergeant
Charles Hilliard-Captain
Joseph Hunter Sr.-Captain
Jesse Jackson-Captain
John Johnson-Captain
Ezekiel Kirtley-Captain
John Kiser-Ensign
David Knight-Corporal
John Knight-Ensign
Samuel Kyle-Captain
Michael Lenon-Sergeant
William Luce-Captain
Jacob Mann-Major
John Mann-Field Colonel
Jacob Mann-Major

John Manning-Musician
John McClary-Lieutenant
David McClung-Sergeant
William McKee-Fifer
Jesse Miller-Sergeant
J. Orr-Lieutenant
Francis Patterson-Captain
John Patterson-Captain
Moses Patterson-Captain
Israel Price-Corporal
Robert Reed-Captain
John Ross-Sergeant
Daniel Rowzer-Sergeant
Benjamin Saunders-Sergeant
John Sheets-Captain
John Shell-Corporal
John Shidaker-Sergeant
Andrew Telford-Sergeant
John Telford-Corporal
Timothy Titus-Captain
John Tullis-Musician
T.B. VanHorne-Colonel
Zebulon Wallace-Corporal
Reuben Westfall-Captain
Michael Williams-Adjutant
John Williams-Captain
Benjamin Winans-Corporal
Lewis Winans-Corporal
Charles Wolverton-Major

BIBLIOGRAPHY

For Sites of Significance.....

<u>A History of Miami County, Ohio</u>.....by The Miami County Sesquicentennial Committee, 1953. Published by F.J. Heer.

<u>A History of Miami County, Ohio</u>.....by W.H. Beers, 1888. Published by W.H. Beers.

<u>Darke County Community Guide</u>.....by the Darke County Chamber of Commerce, 1998. Published by the Ball Publishing Company.

<u>Document Transcriptions of the Old Northwest, Volumes I through XIII</u>.....by Richard Knopf, 1957. Published by the Ohio Historical Society, Columbus, OH.

<u>History of Ohio, Volume III</u>.....by Daniel Ryan, 1912. Published by the Century History Company, New York, NY.

<u>History of Southwestern Ohio, The Miami Valleys</u>.....by William Smith, 1964. Published by the Lewis Historical Publishing Company.

<u>In Search of Fort Nesbit</u>.....by Leo and Arlene Rasor. Published in the Miami County Meanderings, by the Miami County Historical and Genealogical Society, Troy, OH.

<u>Ohio Archaeological and Historical Publications, Volume III</u>.....by the Ohio Archaeological and Historical Society, 1957. Published by F.J. Heer.

<u>Ohio Indian, Revolutionary War, and War of 1812 Trails; Early Road Routes, Formation of Counties, and Military Maps</u>.....By Faye Maxwell, 1974. Published by Maxwell Publications, Columbus, OH.

For Ohio Militia Documents .....
(Publication of Ohio Militia documents fall under public domain rights)

<u>Document Transcriptions of the Old Northwest, Volumes I through XIII</u>.....by Richard Knopf, 1957. Published by the Ohio Historical Society, Columbus, OH.

<u>General Gano's Military Papers</u>.....These papers are in the possession of Cincinnati Historical Society Library. (These are the originals, and have not been microfilmed.)

<u>The Constitution of the Dayton Rifle Company, 1809</u>.....These papers are in the possession of the Troy-Miami County Local History Library, Troy, OH.

<u>The Return Jonathon Meigs Jr. Papers, 1801-1830 (Rolls 1-5)</u>.....These papers are in the possession of the Ohio Historical Society, Columbus, OH.

For Newspaper Articles.....

<u>The Liberty Hall Newspaper, 1812</u>.....Early Liberty Hall newspapers have been microfilmed and are now housed in the Hamilton County/Cincinnati Public Library.

<u>Recollections of the Early Settlement of Miami County</u>.....by Dr. Asa Coleman, 1868. These articles have been published several times in Troy's newspapers and the microfilmed recollections are now housed in The Troy-Miami County Local History Library, Troy, OH.

For Land Bounty Papers.....

<u>Major Jacob Mann and Private Isaac Mann</u>.....Copies of the original papers are in the possession of the author.

Lightning Source UK Ltd.
Milton Keynes UK
UKOW010903051212

203218UK00009B/372/P

9 780788 453366